Slavs to Slavs in Mission

About the Author

David Symon (PhD OCMS) believes in the potential for the Czech Protestant church for intercultural mission and has a deep affiliation for former Yugoslavia countries. He graduated at Charles University in Prague and then, together his wife from Croatia, lived for many years in the Serbian part of Bosnia and Herzegovina. Currently based in the Czech Republic, he teaches missiology and is involved practical work with missionaries.

Slavs to Slavs in Mission
Identity of Czech Missionaries in Former Yugoslavia Countries

David Symon

regnum

Dedication

To my four daughters Jana, Sofia, Pavla and Elizabeta.

Contents

Prologue

I was born in Czechoslovakia and, when I started to attend primary school in our quarter of Prague in 1989, we were obliged to say "Comrade Teacher" until November. Then, we were instructed to switch the address to "Mrs Teacher". Communism fell and, suddenly, many things changed in the country overnight. Other transformations, including the brea-kup of Czechoslovakia into the Czech Republic and Slovakia, occurred more slowly. One instant change was a new-found freedom to proclaim the Christian gospel, as well as the ability to travel abroad without restrictions. This led, among other things, to a gradual rise in international missions from the Czech Republic – at first mainly to the former Soviet Union, particularly Ukraine, and to the former Yugoslav countries.

Historically, missions from the Czech territory have deep roots, whether these were the disciples of Cyril and Methodius, expelled from the Sázava monastery (Eastern Church missions); St Adalbert of Prague (Catholic missions); or the pre-reformers of the 14th and 15th century, including John Hus, and the Moravian brothers (Protestant missions). Despite a relatively rich history, the contemporary Czech Republic is often considered a mission field rather than a missionary sending country. Still, mission activity has increased, particularly in the last decade, as Czech missionaries are being sent with the help of mission agencies or directly as church initiatives. My own background was in an atheist family; I started to believe in Christ at the age of eighteen and almost immediately became involved in intercultural missions. After finishing university studies, I worked in Bosnia and Herzegovina for eight years. Therefore, my interest in the identity of Czech missionaries originates from my personal mission experience, together with questions arising from previous studies in socio-linguistics and practical theology.

Two issues prompted me to explore this topic of Czech mission. The first was my realising the limited degree to which the newly emerging missions from the Czech Republic are accompanied by relevant missiological literature. The second was an attempt to discover how the findings from literature and from Czech mission practice could inform each other.

Czech identity must be understood as an identity constantly re-created and modified. In my search to understand how Czech missionaries negotiate their identity in their interactions with former Yugoslavs I ask:

1. To what extent can the Slavonic Czechs working with their fellow Slavs in former Yugoslavia countries be considered cross-cultural?

2. In what circumstances does the Czech identity of Czech missionaries become salient (that is to say noticed) or suppressed?

3. How does the missionaries' "Czechness" interact with their other identity facets?

This book is a summary of the PhD thesis written on the identity of Czech missionaries and their interaction with Slavs in former Yugoslavia which aims to approach components of the social identity complexity concept and to contribute towards enhancing mission reflection from the Czech Republic. The goal of the research and of the book is to inform mission practice since competencies of missionaries in their inter-cultural work can be connected to their progress in negotiating their identity. This is a pioneer work on Czech mission after 1989 and its exploration may lead towards more publications on identity in connection with mission from Central and Eastern Europe.

Approaching Czech Missionaries

I focus on Czech Protestant missionaries to Slavs in the former Yugoslavia countries since 1989, who were or have been in residence for at least a year or who have been repeatedly returning. The primary sources are the missionaries themselves and others engaged on both the sending and the receiving sides. I used semi-structured interviews, followed by case study thematic data analysis. The interview data was supported by data from personal diaries. These ethnographic elements, such as diary notes and a personal archive of photos, originate from my authentic, yet limited, experience as a mission practitioner.

Because I was able to interview nearly all the known Czech Protestant missionaries in former Yugoslavia countries, I can be confident that my study is without selection bias. There were two streams of primary sources, as I involved missionaries of differing length of mission engagement and supplementary sources, which increased the credibility of the findings.

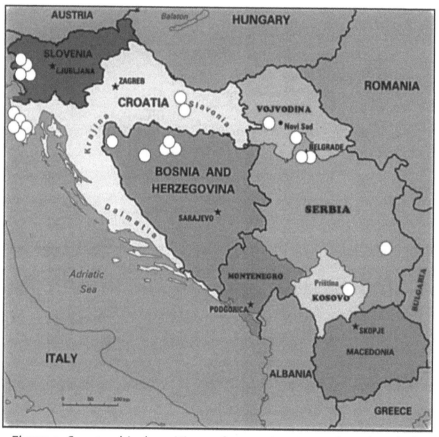

Figure 1. Geographical positions of current, returned, and periodic Czech missionaries in former Yugoslavia countries

As Figure 1 shows, the locations of the missionaries are: Bosnia and Herzegovina (five), Serbia (five), Croatia (seven), Slovenia (four), Kosovo (one). Despite the separate colouring on the map, the Vojvodina autonomous province is counted as part of Serbia. In the overall respondents' statistics, the countries of North Macedonia and Montenegro were mentioned only marginally. One missionary was involved in Kosovo and one missionary family in Slovenia. In Bosnia and Herzegovina, there was one residing missionary and several returning ones. Croatia and Serbia, the biggest former Yugoslav republics, were also the most represented countries in my sample.

The interviewees' names were changed to provide anonymity. When referring to some of their selected responses, to designate a particular country, I applied the United Nations three-letter country codes: BIH-Bosnia and Herzegovina, HRV-Croatia, KOS-Kosovo, MKD-North Macedonia, MNE-Montenegro, SVN-Slovenia, SRB-Serbia.

Introduction of Former Yugoslavia and Czechoslovakia

The name "Yugoslavia" – the land of Southern Slavs (*jug* or *jyz* means "south") – originated in the 19th century, but it was not politically realised until the Kingdom of Yugoslavia came into being in 1929, having replaced the former Kingdom of Serbs, Croats and Slovenes. During the Communist regime of Tito, a specific national category "Yugoslav" was created in the census of 1961 but only a minority of the population identified with the Yugoslav nationality and "yugoslavism" has never been fully realised, remaining only as "yugonostalgia", an overly optimistic picture of the past.

"Former Yugoslavia" refers to the countries of the Socialist Federal Republic of Yugoslavia, which broke apart, in 1991 (Slovenia, Croatia), in 1992 (Bosnia and Herzegovina, North Macedonia), in 2006 (Montenegro, Serbia), and in 2008 (Kosovo). And even though Albanians and other nationals in the region are technically "former Yugoslavs", in this book, the term refers to Slavs whose heritage is rooted in one of these countries. Specifically, these are Bosnians, Croats, Macedonians, Montenegrins, Serbs, and Slovenes.

"Czechoslovakia", on the other hand, consisted of only two nations, and hardly any reference to "former Czechoslovaks" can be found.

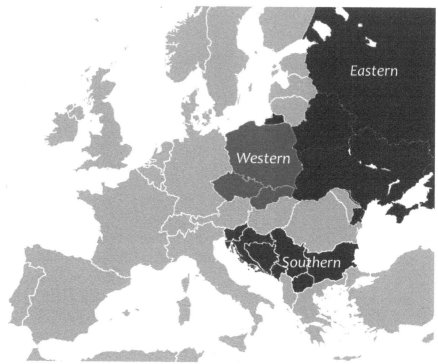

Figure 2. Western, Eastern and Southern Slavs

Czechoslovakia was created in 1918 after World War One, with the goal of constituting a Slavonic majority over the German and Hungarian components in the newly created state. Czechs accepted the common identity more than the Slovaks. After 1989, the country's name was disputed in the "Hyphen War". Slovak deputies insisted on "Czecho-Slovak Republic" and a compromise, "Czech and Slovak Federal Republic" was accepted. Czechs and Slovaks split in 1993 and the Czech Republic and the Slovak Republic (or Slovakia) were formed. The Czech Republic, or the shorter more recently officially recognised version Czechia (Česko) incorporates all three historical regions: Bohemia (Čechy), Moravia (Morava) and Silesia (Slezsko).

In the former Yugoslavia region, there has also been an ongoing discussion on names of particular countries. One of many examples is the name of the Republic of Kosovo, derived from the Serbian word *Kosovo polje* ("field of blackbirds"), and even though it is nowadays inhabited by a majority of Albanians, the Serbian word is used for the country's name, and specifically the ending -o in the English version of the name.

Two Communist Regimes

The Communist regime in former Yugoslavia differed from other countries in Eastern Europe, because the local Communist freedom fighters (*partizani*), not the Red Army, liberated the country from the Nazis, and it was independent of the Soviet Union. The regime was of a gentler nature than in the Soviet bloc, yet the initial purges in 1945 and in 1948 after Tito's split with Stalin surpassed the persecution in some Soviet satellite countries. Since 1948, Yugoslavia pursued a unique self-managed socialism and, throughout the Cold War, led the non-Alignment movement. Yugoslavs were allowed to travel to the West, unlike Czechoslovaks, who were restricted in travel.

Until 1948, the Communist Party of Czechoslovakia's intention was to promote a Czechoslovak form of Communism based on the local democratic tradition. When Czechoslovakia became more anchored in the Eastern bloc, under Stalin's influence, the Czechoslovak's experience of Communism was replaced by political processes in the

1950s. In the "Prague Spring" of the 1960s, the country experienced a loosening of the strict regime, which was stopped by the Warsaw Pact armies' invasion in 1968. The 1970s witnessed hard-line Communist "normalisation".

The fall of Communism in both Yugoslavia and Czechoslovakia was followed by a break-up of the country in the early 1990s along ethnic lines. In Yugoslavia, the organisation of autonomous areas within the country after World War Two had its impact on national self-identification in the early 1990s. Two important factors in this self-identification process proved to be religion and language. Macedonian and Slovenian differ linguistically from the Serbo-Croat language which, because of the political break-up, split into four variants: Serbian, Croatian, and the newer Montenegrin and Bosnian.

Two Break-ups

Czechoslovakia split peacefully, yet the break-up of Yugoslavia was accompanied by the most violent conflict in Europe since World War Two.

Reasons for the violent disintegration of Yugoslavia have been heavily disputed, although the popular view of why "the powder keg of Europe" exploded again is age-long ethnic hatred, connected with the renaissance of religion which strengthened the national movement. But the matter is truly complex. After Tito's death in 1980, the federal party delegated more power to republic parties and allowed decentralisation. Other significant factors were of an economic nature where the more developed republics of Slovenia and Croatia considered themselves held back by the obligation to contribute to the federal budget to support economically weaker fellow-republics. Finally, the re-emergence of nationalism was no surprise after Tito's suppression of it when old wounds from the Second World War re-emerged. Generations changed yet ethnic passions never disappeared. One commentator depicts the operation of "three generations law" when "the grandson tries to remember what the son tried to forget".

While the fall of Communism in the early 1990s meant for most regions of the former Yugoslavia horrific war, Czechs and Slovaks in 1989 after the "Velvet Revolution" on 1st January 1993 experienced a "Velvet Divorce" and the era of freedom, economic improvement, unrestricted travelling and possibilities for international mission work began. The early 1990s were characterised by the return to the European West and the internationalism of civic society. Czech citizens voted in a referendum to join the European Union in 2004. Gradually, the complete openness westwards was replaced by a certain caution, and a split arose between Euro-optimists and Euro-sceptics. This conflict is best depicted by the debate of the two Václavs, the last Czechoslovak (and the first Czech) president Václav Havel and his successor Václav Klaus, who held the presidential office between 2003 and 2013.

Negotiating Spatiality within Europe

Western, Central or Eastern Europe?

Two prevailing views of the Czech Republic now exist, one as part of the West and the other as part of Central Europe. The term

"Mitteleuropa" was reintroduced by Czechoslovak, Polish and Hungarian intellectuals as a tool of "return to Europe", i.e. escaping Eastern Europe. According to the political scientist Ondřej Slačálek, the Czech Republic is clearly Western. He says that it is not a "bridge" between East and West, it represents a West that was merely "kidnapped". In other words, the Czech Republic can be considered as "no more Eastern, but not yet Western".

Although Czechoslovakia was not directly involved in colonial history, a form of Czech colonialism could be the "'development" of the Balkans in the time of Austro-Hungary and the administration of Sub-Carpathian Ruthenia between 1919 and 1939. Although not a Western country – a former coloniser – the present-day Czech Republic shares an indirect responsibility for unequal trade conditions, and by meeting the criterion of belonging to donors of international development aid, and not to receivers, it confirms its belonging to the Global North.

The Balkans or South Eastern Europe?

While "Balkan" is used in English as an adjective, in most Slavonic languages, it is the singular name referring to the peninsula and its political formations. The word *"Balkan"* comes from Turkish and it means a mountain range, formerly Haemus in Greek and presently Stara Planina in Bulgaria. The history of the usage of term "the Balkans" points towards diversified approaches, the main debate being between those who embrace the term and those who disassociate themselves from it, preferring the term "South Eastern Europe".

"South Eastern Europe" is a preferred term particularly in the countries of Slovenia and Croatia with strong links to the West and the EU institutions and a desire to modernise what is considered a periphery of Europe. Its proponents critique "the Balkans" for implying a "unified entity" in their desire to include the region's differences in a more neutral and undefined whole. In this book, I do not avoid the term "the Balkans", but prefer to use "former Yugoslavia countries".

Religious Situation in the Czech Republic

In the 2021 census, 9.3% of Czechia population were Catholic, 1.3% Protestant, 30% with unspecified religious affiliation, and 47.8% without confession. Less than 15% of the population are practising or nominal Christians, and Czechs are proclaimed as one of the most atheistic nations in the world, although one could locate most of today's inhabitants of the Czech Republic in the "grey zone" between a practised religious faith and explicit atheism. They would label themselves as "without confession". Both the Catholic and mainline Protestant churches struggle with decreases in membership, although several smaller Protestant denominations and other minority religious bodies are experiencing growth. There is also a growth in alternative religious movements, and esotericism, eastern philosophy, or new paganism.

Most scholars agree that the 19th and 20th century factors which led to the anti-religious Czech society of today are urbanisation, industrialisation, and liberalisation in the Czech lands. They would also add: the industrial centre of the Austro-Hungarian empire, events of the anti-German and anti-Catholic Czech national revival, anti-clerical interpretations of Czech history after 1918, a shift of a large segment of the population to leftist ideology after the First

World War, and relocation of lower social class settlers to Sudetenland after 1945, when replacing the expelled Germans who were mostly Roman Catholics. Finally, widespread secularism, similarly to the situation in Western parts of Europe, where the church is perceived as irrelevant is also a factor, as well as Communism itself, especially the anti-church politics of the 1950s and the 1970s.

The Czech religious situation differs from other neighbouring countries that also experienced a Communist regime – Eastern Germany, Slovakia and Poland – where statistics show a more positive attitude to religion. Yet, Czechs have strong religious "memory chains" maintained by socialisation and education – and Christianity is the largest official religion historically linked to the country.

The Religious Situation in former Yugoslavia Countries

The ethno-religious matching for Slavs of former Yugoslavia is observed according to the following key: Bosnians are Muslims, Croats and Slovenes are Catholic Christians, Macedonians, Montenegrins and Serbs Orthodox Christians.

Peter Kuzmič, the leading Protestant theologian from the region, comments that national ideologies replaced Communism and he considers this rediscovering of national religious identity to be harmful. Kuzmič argues that Catholic, Protestant and Orthodox churches of Europe are themselves a complex mission field where nominal Christians need to be awakened. Miroslav Volf, Kuzmič's countryman and distinguished colleague, agrees and, to underline the approach in this European context, uses the metaphorical phrase, "washing the face of Jesus", in understanding that Jesus Christ is already present in every culture, even though he may not yet be recognised or worshiped.

Thus, in the Protestant Evangelical view, mission means to reach out to all nations. Nonetheless, in contexts of more traditional Christian established frameworks, the genuine effort of evangelism is often considered an unwelcomed proselytism. Former Yugoslavs share an aversion to proselytism for the reason that it reminds them of the past pressures and fear that it might weaken the fabric of society, which is held together by ethno-religious glue.

For most former Yugoslavs, national and religious identity are interconnected and as such are unchangeable. This is a challenge and has serious implications for the work of Protestant missionaries, including those coming from the Czech Republic.

Identity, Culture, Mission

How do Czech missionaries negotiate their interaction with Slavs in former Yugoslavian countries? This embraces three areas which are interconnected: identity, culture and mission. To comprehend one's mission action, a person's identity needs to be explored, and aspects of their culture of origin investigated. Furthermore, one's identity is moulded by the mission experience and by exposure to other cultures.

Identity

Definition

In identity theory, identity is behavioural and is based on what one does as the role implementer and how one interacts with others. While identity theory focuses on role-based identities, social identity theory's focus is on who a person is as a group member. Henri Tajfel, the founder of social identity theory, claimed that 'It is created out of social realities, it changes with them, it always includes views about "others"'. Social identity theory, based on belonging to a group and on comparison with the "out-group", evolved into social identity theory of intergroup behaviour where groups compete with one another for positive distinctiveness.

Despite the fact that social identity theory and identity theory differ in their understanding of groups, they both address the issue of multiple identities and identity salience, which is important for learning more about the Czech identity of the missionaries and is outlined in the following sub-section.

Multiple identity facets and identity salience

One's social identity is never a final or settled matter. It is complex, and individuals are members of various groups to which they belong at the same time – gender, family, class, occupation, religion, ethnicity and other. In this book, "identities", "identity facets" and "in-group memberships" of Czech missionaries are used interchangeably. Furthermore, the term "identity facets" is preferred to "identities", due to the possible connotation of an unstable and internally split personality that "identities" could evoke. Identity salience is understood by social identity theorists as the activation of an identity in a situation. Analogically, identity suppression can be understood as the likelihood the identity facet is deactivated in a given situation. While "identity salience" refers to situational moments of one's highlighting, noticing, or placing into the foreground a particular identity facet, "identity suppression" means intentional or unintentional deactivating, silencing, turning down, overshadowing, or placing into the background one of the identity facets.

Social identity complexity

The starting point of the social identity complexity is that individuals hold multiple ingroup identities which interrelate. One of the matters this theoretical concept addresses is the nature of the subjective representation of identity interrelations.

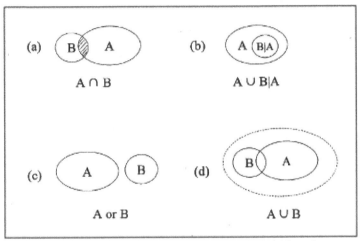

Figure 3. Multiple ingroup representations in social identity complexity

To explain Figure 3, (a) Intersection is a unique identity as an outcome of larger categories from which it is derived, and it is distinct from them. (b) Dominance means that other potential identity facets are subordinated to one primary group identity. (c) Compartmentalisation is the identity representation when context is important – social identities are activated in a specific situation and realised in the process of differentiation and isolation. (d) Merger, as the most inclusive form of social identity, is the sum of all combined in-group identifications. Higher social complexity, when more individuals are perceived as in-group members, is to be embraced as it can help reduce intergroup prejudice.

National identity facet

Ethnicity is one of the most significant group identities. There are two models of looking at the concept of nation: *ethnos* – an ethnic community and *demos* – a state nation. According to Benedict Anderson, who authored "Imagined Communities: Reflection on the Origin and Spread of Nationalism", nations are "imagined" because in the mind of each member there is only an image of the communion with other members; he/she will never meet most of their co-nationals. Nation, nationalism and nation-states are arguably products of modern development, whose origins lie with the Treaty of Westphalia in 1648 and the eighteenth-century French and Industrial Revolutions, or that historical territory, legal-political community and the civic equality of its members are all components of the standard Western model of the nation. On the other hand, others critique the constructivist view by claiming that collective proper name, a myth of common ancestry, shared historical memories, elements of common culture, an association with a specific "homeland" are all attributes of nation as an ethnic community. Both of these conceptions can often be reconciled and situationally both be true for certain people groups in certain time periods.

Christian identity as part of religious identity is closely linked with national identity and leads to theologians who focus on the first century differentiation from Jewish identity as they study the Pauline New Testament letters. A distinctively Christian identity was not formed in that period and is not something which appears at a given moment. William Campbell, an expert on Pauline letters, affirmed that Christian identity is still under reconstruction and urged for its review in the social, cultural, and theological dimensions.

An understanding of Christian identity in this work is based in its perception as an active "Christ-follower" identity, when faith in Christ is connected with deeds that follow, based on a common person, not on common practices and it is not linked to any particular denomination.

Culture

Definition

"Culture", from the Latin word *colere*, can be defined as values, norms, habits, and ways of life characteristic of a coherent social group, or a system of inherited conceptions expressed in symbolic forms by means of which people communicate and develop their knowledge about and attitudes toward life. It can be understood to be a symbolic system by which meanings are expressed in both tangible (e.g., art, gesture, rituals) and intangible (e.g., speech) forms that are socially acquired learned behaviours and are transmitted across generations.

Christian anthropological view of Christ transforming cultures

Many scholars consider Richard Niebuhr's "Christ and Culture" to be a key book that sparked the debate on Christians' approach to culture. Niebuhr proposed a typology with five views of the relationship of Christ and culture: Christ against culture, the Christ of culture, Christ above culture, Christ and culture in paradox, Christ as transformer of culture. His classic work has been critiqued, yet the Niebuhr's type "Christ transforming cultures" is found most helpful by many evangelical authors. Cultures, according to conclusions of the Evangelical statement on mission in the Cape Town Commitment (2010), involve two concurrent elements: appreciation and the need for transformation. There should be no claim to superiority on the part of one's own culture above another culture. In this perspective, cultures are affirmed, yet certain elements within cultures are encouraged to change.

Contextualisation of missionaries in local culture

"Contextualisation" was first used in 1972 at the World Council of Churches to indicate the process involved in integrating gospel and culture in a particular setting. The architects of mission as translation include Andrew Walls, Kwame Bediako, and Lamin Sanneh. Protestant missionaries desire to see the gospel embedded in all cultures and, grounded on the understanding of the biblical verses in 1 Corinthians 9:19-23, they are aware that Christians are obligated to adapt to the culture of others. Still, missionaries tend to base their belief and practices on their home culture and see cultural differences as ungodly. Therefore, it seems that there is an alternative which seeks a balanced approach in which missionary interaction with societies is both true to the Bible and sensitive to the cultures of the particular people groups.

Cross-cultural comparison in missiological perspective

In 1974, the missiologist Ralph Winter addressed the Lausanne Congress for World Evangelism and talked about the urgency of world evangelising shifting the attention from countries as political units to individual nations as ethnic units. In order to mobilise the church to reach the "unreached people groups", Winter introduced the strategic tool of E-scale. In his definition, "E" stands for evangelism, "E-1" means our own culture, "E-2" close culture, "E-3" far culture, in the cultural and not in the geographical sense. Having followed the observation that most missionaries are being sent to "reached" people groups, Winter argued for sending missionaries to E-2 and E-3 cultures until E-1 churches are established. The personal culture of missionaries, caused by their familial and societal background, needs to be taken into consideration as well. There have been missiological attempts to introduce means to measure the extent of distance between cultures. Yet any comparison tool is limited since there is no normative "culture", and therefore it is precarious to compare similarities and differences in a cross-cultural case study.

Mission

Definition

"Mission" has a broad range of meanings, and the usage of the terms "mission" and "missions" is not completely unified. I use it in compliance with those who consider "missions" in plural as multitude of activities that God's people can engage in order to participate in the total biblical assignment – the mission of God. This understanding is linked with the concept of *Missio Dei* when Christians join in God's initiative in mission. "Mission" in this work refers to international or intercultural mission, yet it is not theologically separate from the mission in the home country.

It is important to acknowledge the holistic aspect of mission. The theologian Christopher Wright critiques the "artificially created dichotomy" between evangelism and social action and considers that the Bible provides a warrant for holding the two together. Instead of one or the other holding primacy, he opts for the view of "centrality" when both hub (evangelism) and rim (social action) constitute a wheel of mission.

Mission from the Czech Republic

The topics and concerns of contemporary Czech missiological literature focus on domestic mission in the Czech Republic. Major areas addressed are: (a) ecumenism as means of mission; (b) dialogue with the irreligious majority society; and (c) the relationship between foreign and local Czech workers after the initial influx of Western missionaries to Czechoslovakia and the Czech Republic. On the other hand, the debate on Czech international mission is in its infancy in the Czech Republic.

Contemporary Czech mission to other countries from Protestant churches has been understudied, but some Catholic literature exists. Furthermore, there are several theologians who reflect on mission from countries in Central and Eastern Europe. It is beneficial to gain a broader perspective from related literature, yet it becomes clear that literature on international mission from the Czech Protestant churches is meagre and needs to be enhanced; this book aims to become a part of this endeavour.

Cultural Traits of Czechs and of Former Yugoslavs

This chapter investigates the extent to which the Slavonic Czechs working with their fellow-Slavs in former Yugoslavia countries are cross-cultural. Cross-cultural comparison can be problematic specifically in Central and Eastern Europe where the situation is complicated by the constant change after the economic and social transition.

Five areas emerged as themes from the interviews with Czech missionaries and other respondents: rules vs. people orientation, achievement vs. ascription, individual vs. communitarian, openness vs. closeness, temperamental differences. These were grounded largely in the Trompenaars and Hampden-Turner model of cultural dimensions of cross-cultural comparison.

Rules vs. People Orientation

Order, following rules and procedures vs. certain spontaneity is an area related to how people manage their time. One respondent noticed how people in Bosnia and Herzegovina are more focused on relationships and said that "we Czechs are focused on that something is happening, that things have a flow and move forward, to see some results" (Erika, 1 year in BIH). Others noticed as well that everything has a slower pace in former Yugoslavia countries.

In Bosnian, Croatian, Montenegrin and Serbian languages, there is a phrase *samo polako* (take it easy) which literally means "only slowly". The response of another missionary, Klára, recalls the initial stage of her and her husband's mission stay and their experience was similar to Erika who recognised the difference in the stress on rules, results and activities versus on relationships. For example, while Czechs would perhaps enjoy chatting on the way while walking to some point, former Yugoslavs, enjoy walking back and forth in *čaršija* (the main pedestrian street), as Figure 4 illustrates.

Figure 4. 2003-08 Struga MKD

Time management is connected to efficiency and attitudes to work. The interviewees say:

> *When you plan in the Balkans: 'We'll start at 8 a.m.,' first we get coffee, a cigarette, a relaxed time. [...] It means we meet at eight, but first we rest and so on. In Bohemia, it means the lights are on, we have the tools, and we are working, starting at eight.*
>
> *Dan, returning to SVN*

> *We like to keep the terms and when we make a deal it needs to be valid. Here it is negotiated and almost always it is different than how it was agreed. When you order a plumber on Wednesday at five, then you are literally shocked when you see him on Wednesday at five, mostly he does not come. Mostly he comes on Thursday and in April (laugh).*
>
> *Josef, 20-30 years in HRV*

Dan points out that, in former Yugoslavia countries, work itself first entails the fellowship with co-workers. The matter of not-that-sharp rules concerning the time is taken with humour by Josef, who has adjusted to life in Croatia. It is probably valid that Czechs are more active and hard-working than former Yugoslavs in some areas. Still, it could seem simplistic to mark certain cultures as task-oriented, and other as people-oriented, since all of us are involved in tasks.

Achievement vs. Ascription

While achievement means that the status depends on what a person has accomplished, ascription means that status is attributed by birth, kinship, gender, age or connections. Former Yugoslav cultures are less egalitarian and status is more ascribed than achieved – one such indicator of the importance of prestige is clothes.

Several respondents referred to a rather amusing stereotype of Czechs that former Yugoslavs often utter as they notice Czechs' comparatively lower taste in clothing, which is highlighted by wearing socks in their sandals. One mentioned that he had a friend in Serbia who would go out in the evening, wearing branded clothes to the cost of seven hundred Euros, but he knew that this friend was unemployed. People in former Yugoslavia value outer appearance more and there is also more extravagance in hospitability and fancier celebrations – the occasions could be, for instance, a child's birthday party or a wedding. An anecdote tells of how a Bosnian disgraced his village; while all others would drive a Mercedes or BMW, he came back from Germany in a Škoda Superb. It may sound a bit exaggerated, yet this is often connected to not putting the family to shame.

The strong sense of allegiance to family and friends is connected to the topic of nepotism and corruption in work ethics:

> Some of the Serbian characteristics I don't like because I have tried to start business there and I got angry several times because we talked, we *talked* and there was nothing. So, we tried several times, in different companies, but everyone wanted a commission fee from it.
>
> Radek, returning to SRB

The relationships in that structure appear negative for those out of that culture, it looks like nepotism. For us, who are from this culture it looks like a machine that moves society. It does not have to be positive, neither negative, simply, that's how things work. It depends what kind of person you are, if you build it on biblical ground, knowing that this is not a Western culture, but honour and shame culture, that the patronage exists. It is a habit and here it functions that we take care for each other.

Vladan, pastor and team leader (Kristýna SRB)

In Serbia and most other former Yugoslav contexts, there are situations when Czech approaches, such as Radek's, end in collision. They learn that it is not sufficient to appear on the scene and prove they are good in a certain area (achieved), yet instead they need to know someone (ascribed). This is certainly not connected to specific cultures, but rather systems, especially in the whole post-Communist world. Still, the necessity of a connection to achieve various important or even everyday matters, as Radek was learning, is valid in former Yugoslavia countries perhaps in a larger scale than in the Czech Republic. His frustrated response on work ethics linked with nepotism stands in contrast to Vladan's explanation of positives of the work based on relationships.

There is much strength in such comprehension, as Vladan highlights, yet the side effect is that it discourages individual efforts for achievement, resulting in many young people emigrating to make their fortunes in the West.

Individual vs. Communitarian Culture

In measuring cultural differences, people either regard themselves primarily as individuals or primarily as part of a group. My respondents emphasised the communal aspects of former Yugoslav cultures, such as the significance of the opinion of others, taking care of one another, or simply the value of spending time together. One theme which emerged, linked to practicality and to pragmatism in individualism (vs. communitarianism), is handling money:

> The worst thing you can be in this culture is stingy. If I have money, I want to share. [...] We don't talk about money, how much this costs, how much that costs. If you have money, pay for it.

Diary note from J.V. 2018-07 Sarajevo BIH

Figure 5. 2018-07 Sarajevo BIH

Czechs tend to ensure they are spending the correct amount of money for the quality of the goods or service expected. In Figure 5, Czech short-term missionaries count off the money in the street according to their individual expenses. This contrasts with a more spontaneous way of dealing with money in former Yugoslav cultures, where it is more connected with shame and honour. Economical thinking as a value for most Czechs can be seen as being too thrifty and too concerned for how much one can save. An American missionary colleague who spent twelve years in Sarajevo instructed the Czech short-term mission team during a session on orientation to culture on this mentality: "when you have money, treat others." This can be an expression of privilege and hospitality yet, on the other hand, it may in fact lead to a certain legalism, when taking pride in paying for someone or expecting to be treated next time in return.

Another theme is attitudes toward nature and, according to Trompenaars and Hampden-Turner, there are cultures which see nature as more powerful than individuals, while other cultures incline toward controlling nature. The attitude toward the control of nature is linked to individual responsibility in recycling.

The picture overleaf depicts a container for recycling waste fallen into the middle of River Miljacka in the Bosnian capital, Sarajevo. This is a rather extreme illustration of the comparatively poorer awareness of nature protection and ecology than in the Czech Republic. This is linked to a more individualist stance of the Czech "How can I help recycle?" versus the Yugoslav "Everyone should do it" (and hardly anyone does). As observed in Bosnia and Herzegovina for instance, people highly value cleanliness inside and around their house, yet streets and common places are not that well-kept. This contrasts with a more communal responsibility in this matter in the Czech Republic.

Figure 6. 2009-03 Sarajevo BIH

Czech culture can be considered more individualistic than former Yugoslav cultures. Yet there are both individual elements amongst the Southern Slavs alongside collective elements in Czech culture. Brewer and Chen critique the classical studies of comparison of the West and the East between individualistic and collectivist cultures; they claim that in all societies, individuals are collectivistic and call for a multi-layered attribute of cultures.

Openness vs. Closeness

Czech missionaries perceived a certain openness, or sociability, in former Yugoslavs. They said that they are very cordial and when you meet someone on the street and say: "Let's go for coffee", people are up for it, as opposed to their experiences in Czechia where this would rarely occur. Being able to start a conversation immediately, becoming friends faster and enjoying the hospitability all signify this openness that people from former Yugoslav cultures display more than Czechs. These responses might, however, refer only to the initial level of openness:

> The differences are in that Czechs go for deep water, Croats scratch the surface, and it takes long until you get deep in the relationship.
>
> Josef, 20-30 years in HRV

> Maybe you like to go for a beer, but Bosnians are more kind of a coffee type.
>
> Eldina, supervisor and team leader (Erika BIH)

Josef says that, for Czechs, the first contact might take more time, yet then they often open up, while Croats become friends faster, yet it often is a struggle to deepen the relationship. As Eldina noticed, one culture is more of a beer culture and the other more of a coffee culture. Czechs usually drink beer with friends in the evening after work. For former Yugoslavs, on the other hand, a substantial amount of work is often done over a cup of coffee, sitting with friends during a day in a café.

The Trompenaars and Hampden-Turner model distinguishes between specific cultures (Czech in this case), where work and private life are separated, and diffuse cultures (former Yugoslav), where ideas are not separated from people themselves. There are no sharp edges to it for both cultures are seemingly open in the sense of society. So, instead of finding either Czech or former Yugoslav cultural dimensions to be strictly opened or closed, it seems reasonable to entertain the idea that they are in fact both open and closed, in their own way.

Differences in Temperament

When it comes to describing national temperaments, strong opinions and judgements tended to appear. The general stereotype is that *sjevernjaci* (pejorative term for Northerners in former Yugoslavia) are cold and closed, in contrast to the presumed hospitality, directness, and openness of the Southern nations. On the other hand, Czechs use pejorative phrases such as *horká hlava* (hot head) or *jižní krev* (southern blood), taking pride in their supposedly detached reasonableness in contrast to perceived excessive emotionality. Some Czech respondents said:

> They are different in that they are of fuller temperament.
>
> Erika, 1 year in BIH

> Or one more Croatian, or commonly Balkan, problem comes to my mind that people are split and have disagreements [...]. It is an unhappy characteristic of the Balkan mentality.
>
> Matěj, leader of sending mission agency (Josef HRV)

Czechs tend, quite judgementally, to view the presumed non-tolerating firmness of former Yugoslavs, as opposed to the seemingly refined and polished Czech manners. It is true that the national character of former Yugoslavs is often stereotyped as rather adversarial and linked to "Balkanisation", yet historian Maria Todorova advocates that the "Yugoslav" (not the "Balkan", she emphasises) crisis in the 1990s and its aftermaths ought no longer to be explained in terms of proverbial Balkan enmities and cultural patterns.

Despite the sensitive nature of the judgements, there are still valid elements in statements on the relation of emotions to national temperament. Former Yugoslavs tend to open up more than Czechs in their expressions of joy, sorrow, anger, or national pride.

For instance, flags can be seen not only at sport events, but also on churches or mosques, at weddings and other occasions (Figure 7 is a photo of a Bosnian Serb wedding). Czechs, who are also often

Figure 7. 2017-05 Prijedor BIH

patriotic, find themselves perplexed by this kind of former Yugoslav firm self-confidence which is often linked in their national temperament in an emotional way to their religion.

Even though Czechs tend to be more "neutral", and former Yugoslavs more "emotional", I find it delicate to assess the matter. The findings do point out that there are certain differences in national temperament, yet it probably always depends on one's personal predisposition.

Summary: Different and Similar Cultural Traits

The initial five sections concentrated mostly on the areas of differences. In summary, Czechs, Bosnians, Croats, Macedonians, Montenegrins, Serbs and Slovenes live in a diverse, yet not too distant geopolitical space; they share several common historical epochs; they speak related Slavonic languages; their appearance is similar, they dress like Europeans; they eat, drink and use similar products. Yet in other ways they differ in values and behaviour.

According to the missiological tool of E-scale, for this cross-cultural setting, Czech and the Southern Slavonic cultures could be classified as E-2, i.e. as a "close" culture. Individual perceptions can differ, depending on the region of former Yugoslavia missionaries work in, and their experience. In order to realise in what circumstances Czech identity of the missionaries comes to the foreground or to the background in their ministry and everyday life in the region, this familiarity with basic elements of both cultural environments is required.

Czech Identity of Czech Missionaries – Salient or Suppressed

The Matter of National Identity
Facet Salience and Suppression

"Identity salience", or more precisely "social identity salience", is defined as "the probability that a given identity will be invoked in social interaction", and this depends on factors such as the level of commitment a person has to a particular identity. I am asking: "How and in what circumstances does the Czech identity of Czech missionaries become salient or suppressed?" For Czech missionaries, this includes the broader context of the geo-political location post 1989 and also the interaction with people where their "Czechness" becomes salient or suppressed depending on the situation.

National Identity Negotiation

In 2017 the European Values Study focused, among other things, on the perception of nationality. More than 90% of respondents across Europe viewed nationality in terms of speaking national languages. The importance of political institutions and laws was higher in

Western Europe, while having ancestors in the country or being born there was more prominent in Eastern Europe. The survey results could be connected to a tendency towards an ethnic perception of nation in the Eastern countries, and nation as citizenship in the West. Czechs either possess Czech identity because they have it by birth and ancestry, or because they are citizens of the state and they speak Czech. This has contributed towards an understanding of the complexity of the Czech national salience and suppression.

Czech Identity Salience of Czech Missionaries

Material things as tangible elements of culture are usually noticed by the missionaries in their initial phase of adjustment in the country. One example would be the bus in the picture (Figure 8). While

Figure 8. 2007-07 Gojbulja KOS

Czechia-produced Škoda cars are so widespread that they are hardly noticed in connection to one's "Czechness", other brands such as Zetor (tractors), Tatra (lorries) or Karosa (buses) are much more local. These experiences are connected to what missiological literature refers to as culture shock, described as a "period of confusion and cultural disorientation". This involves a process of learning.

Encountering particular artefacts, such as clothing accessories, meal ingredients, or cigarettes, may come to the foreground in the sense of "I am Czech, I do not wear this, I do not eat this, I do not smoke". Other things may be positive for Czechs enjoy potato-garlic pancakes, garlic soup and other meals which are not enjoyed by former Yugoslavs.

For me, the friendship with my Finnish teammate (Figure 9), with whom I went to the sauna, followed winter sports online, watched a Finnish TV show, listened to Finnish music and ate Finnish food,

Figure 9. 2009-04 Banja Luka BIH

41

meant primarily comradeship and spiritual encouragement, yet also led me to an appreciation of his culture and prompted me to think about my own identity as a Czech.

Czech Identity Suppression of Czech Missionaries

Interaction with non-Czechs

Sometimes encounters with other nationals can have a major influence a long-term exposure leading to the suppression of Czech identity, often during a missionary's stay in their respective former Yugoslavia country.

One respondent recalled that the American team leaders were significant for them. Another had to conform to an American leader who was more experienced as a pastor, yet less experienced as a missionary in Croatia.

Often one particular style of mission is pushed forward, such as an American model of ministry, and the "Czechness" in mission is suppressed. This may be difficult for a missionary, yet Czechs are not that experienced in the contemporary cross-cultural mission work and are often in the position of learners.

Czech language suppression

This is an area when Czech identity suppression, and salience, become obvious. For Czechs, language has historically played a significant role in national self-identification (in opposition to German) and when the language becomes suppressed, national identity is also suppressed. English seems to serve well as a lingua franca for missionary communication and to have an intermediate language is beneficial, yet it may imply a further suppression of Czech. Newbigin complains that "all the dialogue is conducted in the languages of Western Europe, and this in itself determines its terms". Still, missiologists support the value of learning local languages: "If one wants to communicate Christ to a people, he must know them."

Perhaps the most common hybridisation of Czech and former Yugoslav Slavonic languages is in the lexicon. Missionaries who have spent over twenty years in either Serbia or Croatia, when I interviewed them, struggled to find Czech words to express themselves. They employed words in these languages to help them express themselves more clearly. This was helped by the fact that I spoke Croatian and Serbian myself and could "fill in the blanks" for them. Moreover, these long-term missionaries tended to change endings of words and speak with marks of a foreign accent, pronunciation and speech rhythms.

Missionary children who grow up in the mission field find themselves in close contact with the local language. One interviewee at first attempted to speak Czech to her children, yet eventually reconciled herself to Serbian as being the family language. The change took place gradually, although she was aware of the process the whole time. Others initially suppressed their Czech language by a conscious decision to speak exclusively Croatian, even between themselves.

Czech Identity Suppression in Adjustment to the Local Culture

One couple interviewed explained that their daughter got married where they were working and they now have Slovenian grandsons.

Also, the fact that they bought the house, instead of renting, was in line with their long-term calling and ministry. Some of their "Czechness" is perceived as situationally suppressed, as they have settled for life and have culturally adjusted. Yet, no matter if they own a house, or a farm, have a local job, see children intermarry, they still are perceived as Czech both by those around them and in their own eyes. They tend not to think in terms of identity, and suppression of their "Czechness". They prefer to consider the matters practically, in connection to their mission and cultural adjustment.

While returning missionaries, due to the short nature of their stay and relatively low exposure to the local culture, did not seem to struggle with suppression of their national identity, it was an issue for the long-term workers. The goal of one group of missionaries was absorbing the local culture, and yet they were still closely associated with other Czech teammates. They shared that this ambiguity, together with interpersonal issues, resulted in much confusion and was one of the factors leading to burn-out.

The effort of adjusting to the local culture, curtailing their "Czechness" to the background of their identity is not without struggles and it is an ongoing process. Furthermore, it is followed by pitfalls of adjusting too little or too much. Missionaries find it difficult to discern what is cultural and what is supra-cultural. There is a creative tension in the engagement with culture, which includes a certain level of cultural adjustment, and Czech identity suppression. It became clear from the evidence that the suppression of the Czech identity is never complete, it is situational, and it is connected to its salience.

Simultaneous Salience and Suppression
of Czech Identity Facet

Some of those interviewed referred to personality traits, related to cultural differences about achievement and individualism, while others mentioned economic differences and how the Czech Republic is better off than Serbia, with the initial feeling of national pride, based on a better functioning economy.

Some missionaries tend to be very principled with a willingness to suppress their "Czechness", which often became salient through personality, yet there were areas where there was a refusal to suppress habits, including a Czech work rhythm and giving up on speaking Czech. Thus, in the context of mission, there is both an aim for suppression, and putting their "Czechness" aside, yet at the same time wanting to keep, whether consciously or unconsciously what they consider to be their national identity traits.

Thus, the matter of one's social identity is complex, and never final or settled but should be viewed in more dynamic terms. And instead of imagining the identity facets as pistons of an engine moving up and down in a regular fashion, two or more identity facets may become salient at the same time, with varying intensity.

Czech Identity in Mission in Former Yugoslavia Countries

National Identity in Mission

Any serious book on mission stresses the need to suppress ethnocentrism. The very concept of *Missio Dei* entails the understanding that the mission we participate in is God's, and therefore human agents and their identity, including their national identity, are not the focus, where the attention is on other cultures.

On the other hand, emerging missions are encouraged to emancipate themselves and perform missions in their own authentic way across cultures, including those in Central and Eastern Europe. The missiologist Klingsmith says that in the post-Communist region, Polish, Hungarian or Romanian intercultural workers learn to do missions in churches which have in the past held an attitude of inferiority vis-à-vis the West.

The theologian Christopher Wright argued, from Acts 17:26 and Deuteronomy 32:8, that "National distinctives are part of the kaleidoscopic diversity of creation at the human level, analogous to the wonderful biodiversity at every other level of God's creation". Viewed from the biblical perspective, God works with and through nations and ethnic groups – including Czechs. Christians retain these particularities and, according to the missiologist Miriam Adeney, ethnic pride is not necessarily always negative. She compares ethnic pride to a joy parents feel at their child's graduation. It is only bad when exalted as though it were the highest good, which can result in racism, feuds, wars and ethnic cleansing. When ethnicity is treasured as a gift but not worshipped as an idol, God's world is blessed, and we enjoy a foretaste of heaven. The same could be said of national identity.

Czechs and Westerners in Mission in Former Yugoslavia Countries

Czechs' ambiguous spatiality

All Czech missionaries in former Yugoslavia co-operate with other missionaries mainly from Western countries. In contrast to more diverse societies in Western countries, Czechia with its population of slightly over ten million might be considered relatively monolithic but this then can create an even bigger culture shock for a missionary when they are found in such an environment.

The Czech economic situation has changed favourably since the early 1990s, but Czechs still have limited resources. The differentiation from Western teammates is often in financial terms, linked to inferior feelings from forty years of Communist rule which impeded its financial development.

Czechs have been classified as Eastern Europeans yet, again, there are two prevailing views about the position of the Czech Republic, firstly as part of the "kidnapped" West and secondly as part of Central Europe, fittingly encapsulated as "no more Eastern, but not yet Western". After talking to pastors in Serbia and in Bosnia and Herzegovina, I found they both value missionaries who come as helpers, however the relationship to Westerners is ambiguous – both welcoming and reserved.

When considering "the West", those interviewed usually mention Americans and some still refer to the NATO bombing of Serbia in 1999. "Western" certainly does not equal American, yet in minds of Czech missionaries, this often is the first association, perhaps thanks to their personal experience with other mission workers from the USA, who are proportionately quite numerous in the region, and as the result of narratives of the local people, who have had recent experiences with American nationals, mainly the peace keeping forces, during and after the recent war.

Czech missionaries and local workers are sometimes critical of Western missionaries and optimistic about Czech missionaries. Czechs seem to be favoured, as opposed to the Western (and American) out-group, yet the situation is rather complex and differs from person to person. Findings from my interviewees certainly are valid, yet it is simultaneously true that being a missionary sending country for a longer time entails certain procedures of know-how and more self-confidence. On the other hand, Czechs might lack a clear idea of what to do and sometimes become part of foreign mission paradigms.

Czech Identity Salience in Mission

Situational utilisation of Czech identity salience

Figure 10. 2014-04 Banja Luka BIH

When a group from abroad came to Banja Luka, where I worked, they would go out to meet the people, starting conversations and inviting them to events, such as "culture nights" (Figure 10). These were organised by the local church as both educational and outreach in their nature. At one particular Czech culture night before Easter, the presenter had a brief speech about a Czech Easter cake in the shape of a lamb. He explained Czech Easter traditions and bridged it with a Gospel presentation, where the lamb represented Jesus. This is a clear example of the Czech identity being utilised in the mission work context.

Many times, there are unintentional situations of Czech identity salience in ministry emerging naturally. The picture below, Figure 11, documents how a short-term Czech team drew the attention of a national newspaper. Any positive media coverage helps the tiny

Figure 11. 2018-09 Zagreb HRV

Protestant community in Croatia, and the title reads, "Pastor Kreko, with asylum seekers, volunteers and Czechs builds the integration centre". The fact that the Czech team came to help with construction work, where Czechs were "volunteers" along with others, helped draw the attention of the reporter who wrote the article.

The next picture, Figure 12, of the Czech short-term student team illustrates how Czechs, intentionally using their "Czechness", make connections with the local students.

The initial attraction for the Serbian students was that the missionaries, as foreigners, were Czechs. Still, as a result of the familiarity with Czechs and Slovaks with their partners in conversation, the recurring topic they had with local students was the break-up of Czechoslovakia as compared with the Yugoslav experience.

Figure 12. 2016-04 Banja Luka BIH

In the missiological view, there is a legitimate danger of a nationalistic spirit being absorbed into missionary ideology, and highlighting the national identity runs the risk of Christians of a specific nation developing the conviction that they had an exceptional role to play in the advancement of the kingdom of God. On the other hand, there are voices for active usage of one's national traits, calling for their engagement wherever advantageous. Ralph Winter's conclusions for mission strategy as outlined by the E-scale suggest that the utilisation of one's national identity, in the sense of cultural proximity to the target culture, can prove advantageous to mission work. Appropriate utilisation of situational salience of Czech identity facet could help advance the work of Czech missionaries in former Yugoslavia countries.

Acceptance of Czechs by former Yugoslavs

Czechs were accepted across the former Yugoslav areas, although their acknowledgement as Slavs is complex. Czechs, with their twentieth-century experiences of Russian intrusion (since 1945) and invasion (in 1968), are more cautious about pan-Slavonic ideas, or anything which favours Russian hegemony.

The acknowledgement of the independence of Kosovo, the cradle of Serb culture, by the Czech government in 2008 still re-emerges as an occasional stumbling block for individual Czechs in the region.

Favourable factors for Czech missionaries in former Yugoslavia countries

Czechs have not caused historical harm in former Yugoslavia; therefore, they are likely to be received favourably. Czechs might not have led wars, occupied a territory or colonised an underdeveloped country, nevertheless, an attitude of invaders might be reflected in the mission work of anyone with incorrect motives. History, often underestimated by Evangelical Christians, seems to play a significant role in acceptance of individual nationals. In spite of certain grey areas, elements in Czech history are beneficial for Czech missionaries.

The four decades of communist rule (1948-1989) left their marks on the Czech national character: "The Czech person was taught not to say too much, not to ask too much, not to care too much, not to be bold, creative, or innovative". As the result, several characteristics prevail: distrust of authorities and institutions, distance from formalised religion, a flawed work ethic and personal character, a poor approach to responsibility in public and private sectors, cynical humour as a tool to oppose imposed dogmas, and pessimism and feeble national self-confidence. The Czechs are a nation of ten million which for long periods of its history were ruled by someone else. Czechs have been accustomed to adjust to others and still have to adjust, particularly when they travel abroad as they cannot expect anyone speak Czech. Czechs, together with others in post-Communist countries, have also experienced lower living standards and have learned to adapt.

From South-Eastern Moravia, it is only three hundred kilometres to the Slovenian border, while from the Western-most tip of Bohemia, it is one thousand seven hundred kilometres to the remotest part of North Macedonia. The journey to most places of former Yugoslavia countries can be easily carried out from the Czech Republic by car in one day.

Whether the Balkans is an "ideal" mission field for Czechs is questionable; nonetheless, the following could be favourable factors for Czech missionaries in the former Yugoslavia region:

a Slavonic cultures and languages are close

b equality factor: Czechs used to be economically poorer

c Yugoslav familiarity with Czechs and a partial common history

d no historical harm

e geographical proximity

f Czechs' presumed trait of adjustability

Czechs' advantages in mission depend on an individual missionary's personal dispositions – character, commitment, talents and gifts, previous experiences and other factors. The starting position of being Czechs, i.e., their national identity, is only one aspect for "effective" mission in former Yugoslavia.

Following the war in the 1990s, former Yugoslavia countries experienced two trends: increased conversion rates to Protestantism and an influx of foreign missionaries. Consequently, the newer churches, who make up a small minority, have often been looked upon with suspicion as a foreign threat and intrusion or are labelled "sects".

Challenges of ethno-religious identity
for Czech Protestant missionaries

The status of Protestants in former Yugoslavia countries differs from the Czech context where it is the widely accepted form of Christianity. Peter Kuzmič explains that, in the former Yugoslavia countries, Protestant minorities are looked upon with suspicion as a radical movement which in past divided Christendom and currently, in its fragmented forms, threatens national and religious identity and people's unity. Muslim or Catholic and Orthodox Christian bodies are often unwilling to be open to alternative expressions of faith in their "canonical territory" due to their religious and national identity.

The picture above of a billboard on a bus station in a town centre (Figure 13) illustrates an example of a radical nationalist manifestation, connected to religion. It says: "Serb, do not forget. Christ is risen. Kosovo and Metohija [old Serbian name for the

Figure 13. 2010-04 Laktaši BIH

Western part of Kosovo] has always been Serbia". The connection of the two identity facets is not something which only the older generation hold onto – a survey among youth in the Western Balkans recently confirmed that "ethnic and religious identities are overlapping". Thus, Bosnians are Muslims, Croats are Catholic Christians, Macedonians are Orthodox Christians, Montenegrins are Orthodox Christians, Serbs are Orthodox Christians, and Slovenes are Catholic Christians.

The religious identities usually signify ethnic, cultural and political orientations rather than being linked to the Christian gospel as such. Protestant Christians are often the ones who use the expression "biblical", in order to point out they are right, while others are not, yet this does not imply the Bible is not held in high esteem and usage in the Catholic and Orthodox circles in former Yugoslavia countries.

One extract concludes this section on how ethno-religious identity presents a genuine challenge for the work of Protestant, Czech and other missionaries in former Yugoslavia countries:

> In spring, an article [Figure 14] appeared in the local leading newspaper headed: "Jehovah's witnesses are again knocking on the door". One third of the article focused on our local Evangelical student movement, local branch of International Fellowship of Evangelical Students. Later in July, a state TV made an interview with myself and my colleagues about "various student movements in the town", I learnt the day it was broadcast it meant "the cults in the town".
>
> Diary note from D.S., 2013-07 Banja Luka BIH

Figure 14. 2011-11 Banja Luka BIH

Figure 14 shows the newspaper article, entitled "Secret religious rituals in flats", documents the diary note above and the widespread generalisations in Bosnian Serb society, which is present across former Yugoslavia countries. One man referred to the only Slovenian region influenced by the Reformation, which otherwise had a little historical impact in the whole region. Contemporary Protestant missionaries consider themselves to be entitled to carry on the mission, which for the Evangelicals means proclaiming the gospel to all nations regardless of the jurisdiction. While on the other side, for the traditional ecclesiastical bodies, mission is focused on believers in diaspora and on preserving the national identity. In former Yugoslavia, "Islam, Roman Catholicism, and Eastern Orthodoxy all consider this an auspicious time for the re-activating and re-educating the people in their spheres". In this way, the institutionalised religion, like nationalism, has ambitions to supply existential answers to peoples' quests for security, totality, and wholeness.

Still, the Protestants might have created other obstacles, for the small size of native Protestant churches in former Yugoslavia countries implies a higher proportion of foreign missionaries and, together with them, a natural influence of other cultures.

The picture overleaf (Figure 15) shows a poster inviting university students to a "Concert of Christian music" by a Czech short-term team. Many Serbian students, who were invited, avoided it as a cultic thing. They considered Christian music to be choir music in a church building, not a bass guitar and drums accompanied concert in a club setting.

Many churches were established by the missionaries and, in Kuzmič's words, they are frequently considered as "a modernised Western faith, and thus a foreign intrusion". As the result of this, these churches sometimes tend to get Westernised. Newer Protestant churches in the Balkans are often a unique meeting points of multiple cultures, when not being burdened by nationality, this is seen as a positive contribution towards reciprocal reconciliation. This diversity, which says that Jesus' church transcends all cultural and language barriers, might appear to the local religious bodies as a treacherous "transnational faith", a threat to the security of ethno-religious identity.

Figure 15. 2011-11 Banja Luka BIH

As such, there are multiple challenges, both external and internal, which emerge in mission work.

Towards a dialogue concerning ethno-religious identity

To choose for oneself and to embrace something different than the national mainstream religious belief is often considered a foreign concept, not compatible with the national historical pride. Moreover, there is a mentality of: "Why would we convert now in peace when we did not convert under the pressure of war?" and conversion can indeed be regarded as treason to the nation itself. This observed inclination is nonetheless not a permanent state of affairs.

Nick Vujičić is a world-known Australian motivational speaker and evangelist of Serbian origin. One major side-effect of his ministry is a positive public relation for Protestant churches, for "If this great Serb can be a Protestant Christian, they are not that a dangerous sect after all." However, this view is not shared by everyone. Czech Protestant missionaries find themselves periodically struggling with the ethnoreligious identities of former Yugoslavs. On the other side, as the following statement shows, they highly appreciated some of its elements:

> I think it is easier to talk about God. On one hand, it's a disadvantage that they are all Orthodox here, on the other side, there is advantage they have a notion of God, so if a person brings that topic, it is not completely off. They follow on that, we start to talk, and ask, and you are not a completely strange person. In Bohemia, we would be for some people totally off, what are we talking about.
>
> *Ema, 2-10 years in SRB*

The widespread cultural Christianity and familiarity of most people with its basic beliefs, due to the ethno-religious environment, enables people to converse about God more openly, without the estrangement which is present in Czech society. Another element is the awe of God, which influences for the better moral matters, such as crime and safety. Slovenia, as opposed to the rest of former Yugoslavia, is often considered a traditionally Catholic country, yet has a strong secular humanism and "liberal" anti-Catholic element in the society.

Nevertheless, the religious situation in the Czech Republic and in former Yugoslav republics differs significantly. In the European Values Study in 2017, the percentage of people who said religion was very or quite important in their lives was: Czech 21%, Slovenia 37%, Croatia 64%, and other former Yugoslav countries were around 80%. Only 38% of Czechs claimed they believed in God, while in Bosnia and Herzegovina and Montenegro it was about 96%.

Mission in two directions

The focus here is on Czech missionaries to former Yugoslavs, but due to the nature of religious identity in both contexts, I conclude a twofold mission is possible: from the Czech Republic to former Yugoslavia countries; and from Bosnia and Herzegovina, Croatia, Kosovo, Montenegro, North Macedonia, Serbia, and Slovenia to the Czech Republic.

In former Yugoslavia countries, the Evangelical church is less viable. There are areas with no Christians altogether and all Protestant churches are indeed tiny, perhaps with the exception of the Northern Serbian province of Vojvodina. Viewed comparatively, the Czech Republic seems to be in a better position regarding access to the message of Christ. The Evangelical church, even though it is by no means gigantic, is sizable and more legitimate in society. From the point of view of Czech missionaries, they come from a better-off place with something to offer. Nevertheless, it is the Czech Republic which usually is the number one country in prayer booklets on reaching the irreligious representing an "Atheistic world".

From this viewpoint, apart from those Protestant Evangelical missiologists who would agree that Muslims of former Yugoslavia need a chance to be presented to the Jesus in the Gospels, non-religious Czechs with a distant conception of Christianity need to be evangelised, and formally Christian southern Slavs need to be evangelised, or re-evangelised, since the ethno-religious identity often prevents them from clearly distinguishing what is Christian and what is part of their national tradition.

Czechs can evangelise and inform the former Yugoslav ethno-religious identity. Freedom to change confession can be precarious in any culture, for family reasons, yet it seems that in the Czech Republic, it is more widespread. This is not merely connected to a more individualistic way of life – as Newbigin accentuates, it in essence represents the Christian doctrine of freedom which "includes both the ability to hold vital convictions that lead to action and also the capacity to preserve for others the freedom to dissent". So, while in the predominantly ethno-religious context former Yugoslavia there is need for closure – for example to be a good Croat you need to be Catholic – Czechs have adopted more liberal perspective of low group membership overlap – you can be Czech and believe in anything. In connection to that, the Protestant church, unlike in the Czech Republic, tends to be viewed as a Western import. Similarly, a healthy self-identification process can be embarked as former Yugoslavs ask what it means to be let's say, a Serb Protestant.

Former Yugoslavs with their ethno-religious identity can evangelise Czechs and inform Czech believers on their Christian identity. In former Yugoslavia countries, the starting point that there is a God can be a huge step forward and an advantage. Most Czechs do not accept God's existence, even though they celebrate Christmas and Easter. With help, Czechs could actually be informed about the meaning of these holidays and celebrate them properly. South Slavs are more festive and, due to the glue of ethno-religious identity, the whole society is included in the preparation for holidays – e.g., fast, time of mourning before Easter Sunday, esteem for the saints of history, stress on the time family spends together. One cannot generalise for all Czechs, since many do celebrate national holidays in keeping with their meanings. Still, most often, Czechs "celebrate" by merely appreciating a day off work.

Interrelations of "Czechness" with Other Identity Facets of the Missionaries

Introducing Identity Facets of Czech Missionaries

Social identity is complex, and all individuals are members of various groups at the same time. Group membership provides them with a certain social identity. This identity is sometimes classified as primary or secondary. The sociologist Anthony Giddens said: "Apart from being human, which is a first unexpressed and anticipated component of self, primary identities are those connected to primary socialisation processes in the early stages of life: gender, race/ethnicity and perhaps also disability." There cannot be strictly delimited "primary" or "secondary" identities and single identities can be approached interchangeably, e.g. family membership, class, or religion can in some societies be ascribed, while in others achieved.

Both identity theorists and social identity theorists agree that the overall self or one's identity is organised into multiple identities or identity facets, and each of them is tied to aspects of the social structure. The sum of these multiple "social identifications" describes one's overall social identity. A useful phrasing could be "shape" or "contribute towards forming". Scholars propose multiple bases to one's identity: individual self-concept for personal identity, expectations tied to social positions for role-based identity, social group membership for social identity. In my analysis, these were intermingled, and complex.

These were the tentative categories discovered for Czech missionaries (apart from their Czech national identity facet): male or female, family member, personality traits holder, interest group member, worker, Christian worker, Christian, missionary, someone with regional or supranational identity, and identity facet of other national. This arrangement emerged by employing thematic analysis on the case study of Czech Protestant missionaries, who were interviewed between 2018 and 2019, and admittedly this list cannot be considered as a definite and complete. Rather, it serves as a starting point.

The Four Social Identity Complex (SIC) Interrelations as the Analysis Framework

This chapter focuses on the subjective representation of the four identity interrelations of social identity complexity – intersection, dominance, compartmentalisation and merger. To add to the diagram outlined earlier (Figure 3), intersection and dominance are assigned a relatively low-complexity, and compartmentalisation and merger a relatively high-complexity. Social identity complexity concept has been used mainly on the multicultural contexts, as a tool for peaceful cohabitation and reducing prejudice, yet it has been also applier more widely in other cases. So, to answer, "How does the missionaries' 'Czechness' interact with their other identity facets?", this chapter investigates:

- Which of the four interrelations of identity facets fit the Czech missionaries the most?
- Do Czech missionaries possess low or high complexity?
- Would higher complexity lead to better missionary adjustment in South Slavonic cultures, contribute to lowering mutual outgroup prejudices and have a positive effect on missionary work?

Intersection

Intersection – that is to say applying diverse group identities into a single social identity of two differing national identities – was found by some as disorienting:

> *After some time, we blended. It is stupid somehow, you do not feel you are a Czech, at the same time you are not a Croat, and you are something in between [emphasis added]. That is a very odd feeling. And when we came back, we noticed some faults of the Czech culture because the Croatian culture is far ahead in some things and you feel unpleasant in your own culture and you are ashamed of it, but you have to live here now.*
>
> *Renata, 10-20 years in HRV*

Renata admitted she no longer felt Czech but not yet Croatian and used the words "something in between" which suitably describe the SIC category of intersection. "Crisis of identity" was how the missionaries in Slovenia worded it. The missionaries, often struggle in the identification process and a personal crisis might occur.

Another missionary also found it conflicting, yet he has gradually been learning to reconcile the two and acknowledge this intersection position.

Roccas and Brewer specify a term "integrated biculturalism" which, unlike compartmentalisation, acknowledges multiple cultural identities simultaneously. It might more fittingly classify as the SIC category of merger. It gets more complicated by the presence of more national identity facets. These multidimensional intersections vary substantially with each missionary.

Dominance

Dominance is another form of interrelation of ingroup memberships when inconsistencies are suppressed. In case of the "Czechness" of the missionaries, it can either dominate or be dominated. The most significant theme for SIC interrelation of dominance, was the superiority of the Christian identity. Apostle Paul shares with the Gentiles that, for Christians, the primary identity-marker is faith in Christ. This identity facet emerged for Czech missionaries in situations of encounter with other nationals, especially within the context of common time of worship and prayer, as one worker, Radek explained: 'When I experience the unity with them, it is in prayers.' He realised that it did not matter where they were from, that some were Czechs and others were out-group – in those moments of experiencing spirituality together, they all were in-group, uniting in the dominant overreaching Christian identity.

Missionaries consider the suppression of "Czechness" to the dominant Christian identity a desired goal. The matter of setting aside the Czech identity is, nevertheless, highly problematic, no matter how purposeful a missionary's practice is. Patrik and his wife were not able to delineate themselves from the national identity facet, yet Patrik's perspective is that for them this identity is not the top priority. For him it was being a Christian, being a pastor, being a church planter.

The statements of the missionaries in this section revealed a dominance of Christian identity in the sense of transcending, but not replacing the national (or other) identity facet. It appears more legitimate to view the dominating Christian identity as not cancelling, but rather transcending, all other identities.

Compartmentalisation

Compartmentalisation implies dividing identity facets into single compartments which occasionally come to the foreground. Such as a certain type of behaviour in social contacts, such as stress or in-group threat. The contexts can be various historical, cultural and religious situations, and personal relationships. For Czech missionaries, this broader context is after four decades of communist rule, since 1989.

Compartmentalisation refers to identity salience – while one or more identity facets are activated, others are muted, yet not completely abolished. One respondent lives out their Czech identity when in Serbia and their Serbian identity when in the Czech Republic. Another one shared something similar for Croatia. For them, the context of their current location determines that the other national identity facet becomes activated. I record in my diaries that, in the context of an international conference where I came from Zagreb with a group from Croatia, I identified with Croats and with other students

Figure 16. 2004-04 Györ HUN

from former Yugoslavia countries. There was a Czech group present as well, yet I hardly spent any time with them; the picture below (Figure 16) documents a reunion gathering of delegates from former Yugoslavia countries.

One used to write his prayer update or newsletter, in Czech for Czechs and then in English with one version for his American and the other for his Japanese supporters. Retrospectively, he viewed this very negatively and for such a compartmented way of missionary practice used the word "schizophrenia". This discrepancy in the situational identity salience was one of many factors leading to his burn out, as he admitted in the interview.

Compartmentalisation of a single identity facet can both be beneficial and demanding, depending on personal situation of each missionary.

Merger

Merger resembles compartmentalisation, nevertheless the conjunction "or" is replaced by "and" for the reason that "differences are recognised and embraced in their most inclusive form". It is the highest possible representation of how one's ingroup memberships interact, and often appears to transcend single categorical divisions.

When asked about moments when he suppressed his "Czechness", one of the respondents answered:

> *I did it most of the time. I did not perceive that I am a Czech and they are from another culture. I was always trying to speak their language, to use the thing they use, eat the same food they eat.*
>
> *Marek, 1 year in KOS*

This missionary in Kosovo seemed to embrace his identity facets in their most inclusive form, as he viewed his national identity with blurred edges. He did not perceive he was Czech and they were Kosovo Albanians or Serbs. That does not mean that he was not aware of it at all, yet he avoided categorisations if not necessary.

A son of long-term missionaries, who grew up in Slovenia, instead of being assigned to Czech or Slovenian identity, jokingly suggested his identity was derived from his parents. This can either be a sign of insecurity or it can mean that they embrace all identities and do not need to categorise themselves.

Merger, by its definition preserves both differentiation and integration in an inclusive social identity. Some of the responses point to both insecurity and refusal of Czech missionaries to think in the categories of individual identity facet. Nevertheless, they all perceive their identities as integrated, and this is linked to the SIC interrelation of merger.

There is often a reciprocal relation of merger to other SIC interrelations. One of those interviewed desired his primary national identity to be switched from Czech to Croatian, yet he found himself in a place of intersection. Gradually, he became more confused, and this was one of the factors leading to his burn out. Another realised that it is useful to adapt to the local environment, yet realised that elements of his original identity could be kept and held in a healthy balance, emphasising that keeping national identity is important in order not to erase the intercultural dialogue. Kristýna expressed a spiritual viewpoint, saying:

> I think that, as a missionary, you have the advantage to take from each culture the good things. [...] And our country is really heaven, inhabitants of God's kingdom.
>
> Kristýna, 20-30 years in SRB

In summary for Czech missionaries and others in former Yugoslavia, their multiple identity interrelation often appears to be as intersection or compartmentalisation, yet the ideal they aim at is merger, with an attached dominance of Christian identity facet.

The ability of Czech missionaries to embrace the differing cultural elements of former Yugoslavs and to manage the situational salience of "Czechness" thus seems to depend more on personal predispositions, such as character traits, rather than solely on a skill in interrelation of the multiple identity facets they hold. The humble stance of an integrated (merger-like) identity of a missionary is an attribute which is not always present. The ideals that "missions must flow out of mission, which means we have no missional authority apart from the mission of the triune God" and that mission is supposed to be a "humble prophetic dialogue" are not always truly embodied.

Missiological Implications of Social Identity Complexity

This leads to implications for mission practitioners, as they can benefit from their self-understanding and from reflection on their social identity, in terms of ingroups and outgroups, and on their role-related identity. From a missiological perspective, a more integrative treatment of one's identity facets is a suitable goal for intercultural work. Paul Hiebert in the mid-1980s used similar terminology to that introduced by Roccas and Brewer in 2002 for the identity of missionaries who live in-between their own and their local culture. He critiqued both "rejection" and "compartmentalisation" and encouraged "integration" as the most suitable model for identity negotiation.

I conclude that high social complexity functions better for the Czech missionaries: "Czechness" as one of many identity parts becomes salient in certain contexts (compartmentalisation) or is included in the whole (merger). On the other hand, the less complex forms of identity interrelations, functioning more as a fixed identity, could be potentially harmful for the mission work. Intersection could imply an unwillingness to be changed by the mission field experience and by the non-Czech outgroup. Dominance could be even more harmful when a situational threat of Czech ethnocentrism might become a barrier for the missionary work.

The more singular forms of identity could potentially be detrimental for the mission work and higher identity complexity, when a missionary is open to adjust and learn, can be beneficial for the advancement of missions. Czech missionaries do not possess either low or high complexity, yet the identity facet interrelation the missionaries should settle, is merger, with dominance of Christian identity facet as a transcending element.

Being a "missionary"

One particular identity facet the respondents seemed to address a lot was "missionary". This identity facet seemed to appear inappropriate, on many occasions, in lands with Christian heritage. The longer Czech Protestant missionaries stayed in one of the former Yugoslavia countries the more they refused to be categorised as missionaries and a shift towards a more effective adjustment took place. While only one missionary couple seemed to identify themselves with it and considered themselves "pioneering missionaries", others expressed varying levels of disassociating from being a missionary.

One young married woman stated: "I am not a missionary, I went to follow my husband, but I have no calling to mission." Her husband Jonatán was the missionary and she, not that excited about the move from the Czech Republic, rejected any association with it – both the missionary label and function. Yet, she served in the church in her free time, along the tourist guide job. It, nevertheless, seems that gradually they both managed to soften the sharp edges of their initial identity delineation. Jonatán also has started to work in tourism, and instead of typical "missionaries", they pursued radiating the Gospel of Christ while working with people interculturally.

Another worker, Patrik, was assessing his businessman identity, along or instead of the missionary identity, which depicts well something most missionaries in former Yugoslavia go through: They negotiate their status and usually there are one or more elements that not only legitimise their stay in the eyes of many local people but allow them to develop their gifts and abilities and to serve the community in a practical way. Later in the interview, Patrik added:

> We are primarily not missionaries, understand, of course we do belong to that category, on ground of that we went from one country to another, yes, *but* we didn't say: "Now we'll be missionaries." The Lord God gave us on our heart Jablonec [in northern Bohemia], so we went to Jablonec and planted the church. And it was mission too, even though it was mission in our own culture.
>
> Patrik, 20-30 *years* in SVN

He refused to be categorised as a missionary and referred to the artificial division between evangelism and "mission". He has been seriously reconsidering the approach to the missionary identity and so did others, who have spent over twenty years in a former Yugoslav country:

> I feel certainly Czech, a Czech who has accepted Croatia as his country. I definitely don't perceive myself as being on a visit here. I will remain Czech, but this is my home. We didn't say we are missionaries here; we are immigrants.
>
> Josef, 20-30 years in HRV

I have come to mission to serve God here and I am a God's servant. When you say "missionary" it is kind of cold.

Kristýna, 20-30 years in SRB

Both Josef and Kristýna explicitly did not identify with being "missionaries". Their rootedness in Croatia and Serbia, yet still with ties to the home country and to other Czechs, reflects how missionaries are insiders and outsiders at the same time. According to missiologist Paul Hiebert, missionaries "acquire an international perspective and the ability to adapt to more than one culture, but at the price of being fully adjusted to none of them." It seems as if the self-identification shifts from a missionary identity of those who visit regularly or spend their first years in the country to a more non-missionary identity. The longer the missionary spends in the country, the less of a "missionary" remains in his identity. With these missionaries, a certain shift towards more effective adjustment took place, and it was expounded by a more comprehensive self-perception of the missionaries – and a more complex social identity.

Summary

My findings showed that Czechs are, in some respects, culturally similar to Bosnians, Croats, Macedonians, Montenegrins, Serbs and Slovenes. They speak related Slavonic languages; their appearance is similar, they dress like most Europeans; they eat, drink and use similar products. Yet, their cultures differ. They differ in values and behaviour, and in their national temperament. Such cultural proximity is to be placed as E-2 on Ralph Winter's E-scale.

The evidence of Czech missionaries showed that their national identity is a dynamic process which has an internal and external aspects and becomes salient or suppressed either intentionally or unintentionally, in different situations. It also differs as to whether the missionaries perceive their identity, such as "Czechness", for themselves or how it appears to others.

The Czech national identity facet of the missionaries is related to other parts of their identity facets: intersection – being disjointed in-between two national identities; dominance – domination of Christian identity facet; compartmentalisation – in settings and situations of Czech identity salience; or merger – integrating the differences in cultural adjustment.

Missiological Findings and Implications for Mission Practice

The thesis of this book and of my fuller PhD is that awareness of Czech national identity provides a tool for reducing missionaries prejudice in their effective contextualization in former Yugoslavia countries.

I concluded that, in ideal situations, high social complexity signifies prerequisites for better adjustment and functioning of missionaries, as it contributes to lowering mutual outgroup prejudices and positively affects missionary work. On the other hand, the less complex forms of identity interrelations, or the more singular forms of identity, could be potentially harmful for the mission work. One such example is that many found the missionary identity facet unfitting in lands with Christian heritage. It was evidenced for Czech Protestant missionaries that the longer they stayed in one of the former Yugoslavia countries the more they refused to be categorised as missionaries.

Beneficial salience of "Czechness"

The effort of contextualization entails the suppression of national identity of the missionaries, but it is never a complete process for, whether consciously or unconsciously, they the missionaries keep components of their Czech identity facet. Czech missionaries, or alternately other foreign missionaries, are to be attentive to their national identity facet, due to its impact on their conduct in a foreign environment, which they seek to influence missionally. This can immensely help them to prepare for mission work in an intercultural context, to daily function in the mission field, and to experience a healthy return to their sending country, which is often a problem as mission practice confirms.

So, I found that adequate management of situational salience of the national identity facet can help advance the work of Czech missionaries in former Yugoslavia countries, but this does not comprise a Czech identity in a nationalistic sense. In a missiological view, there is a highly relevant orientation in suppressing one's identity, including national identity, to identify with those the missionary serves. There is a legitimate danger of nationalistic spirit being absorbed into missionary ideology as mission theologian David Bosch warns: "Christians of a specific nation would develop the conviction that they had an exceptional role to play in the advancement of the kingdom of God through the missionary enterprise." Still, when treated correctly as a situationally salient national identity facet, it can serve as a beneficial asset for the advancement of the mission work and my findings revealed positives of the "Czechness" of the missionaries in the context of former Yugoslavia countries.

This material on Czech identity facet displayed the search for an authentic Czech way to participate in global (worldwide) missions, while not merely adjusting to the Western-missionaries-dominated patterns in international teams. Those who worked in international teams, were in most cases influenced or led by Americans and the team language was English. This meant a double cultural adjustment and two languages to learn. Yet it also implied that Czechs, who are not that experienced in contemporary cross-cultural mission work, have started to ask for self-identification – "What does it mean to be a Czech in missions?" This exhibited Czechs' self-identification process, which is in progress in newly emerging missionary-sending nations. It is contributing by its minor, yet proportionately corresponding, share to the mosaic of the global Christian mission movement.

Favourable factors for Czechs in former Yugoslavia countries

Czech missionaries possess these favourable factors in what was assigned as E-2 culturally proximal context: Slavonic cultures and languages are close, equality factor; Czechs earlier were economically poorer than former Yugoslavs; familiarity with Czechs and a partial common history; no historical harm; geographic proximity; Czechs' presumed trait of adjustability.

These factors can serve as a fuel for an optimistic view for Czech mission, yet have to be approached carefully. I noticed that Czechs seem to favour themselves, and so did Southern Slavs, in opposition to their Western missionary colleagues, yet the situation in reality is rather complex and differs in individual cases.

Potential for mission in two directions

Due to the nature of religious identity in both contexts, a twofold mission is possible – Czechs to former Yugoslavs and former Yugoslavs to Czechs.

I argued for a twofold mission:

   a. Czechs can evangelize former Yugoslavs and inform their ethno-religious identity. There is space for freedom of choice to change confession could be validated, with the capacity to preserve traits of national identity. Unlike in the Czech Republic, the Protestant church is often viewed as a

Western import in countries of former Yugoslavia. This could change due to commencement or deepening of the self-identification process of former Yugoslav Protestants.

b. Former Yugoslavs, with their ethno-religious identity, could evangelise irreligious Czechs and inform Czech believers about their Christian identity. First, most Czechs are "believers in something", and they do not share with former Yugoslavs the starting point of general awe of God which influences the moral. Second, Czech evangelical believers can be reminded of matters of Christian tradition, namely observance of Christian holidays and to perhaps learn to collectively celebrate it.

These conclusions are in accordance with the notion that the mission field is omnipresent. The focus of my research was Czech mission agents and their identity, yet this mission from everywhere to everywhere involves mission both to former Yugoslavs, and to Czechs. The paradoxical finding was that Czechs could themselves be evangelised, or re-evangelised, by former Yugoslavs, whom, due to their ethno-religious identity, their fellow Czechs (Protestant Evangelical missionaries, as documented in my work) consider in need of the Christian gospel and to whom they develop their mission effort.

Based on partial findings on national identity negotiation in relation to religious identity in both cultural spheres, I suggested that evangelism or re-evangelism is required, and intercultural mission could be performed in the two directions – Czechs (from whichever church affiliation) to former Yugoslavs, and former Yugoslavs (from either Protestant, Catholic, or Orthodox circles) to Czechs. Such mission endeavour, appropriately accompanied by mission reflection, could significantly contribute to the global Christian mission.

Further Prospects for the Topic

There is room for initial research on Protestant (and perhaps other Christian) mission from former Yugoslavia countries. Former Yugoslavs presumably share with Czechs similar beneficial factors for mission to similar contexts, including familiarity with the culture or similar language. No matter how small the emerging Protestant mission from former Yugoslav countries is, it could still be addressed in missiological literature. What seems familiar are individual missionaries from Vojvodina province to the Southern parts of Serbia and to Montenegro, and also missionaries from Croatia and from Serbia to Bosnia and Herzegovina after 1991. During the course of my writing, I have witnessed new former Yugoslav missionaries leaving for another non-former Yugoslav country as full-time missionaries, a continuous mission to the Roma, and the rise of mission to the refugees who have been transiting through the Balkans since 2015.

There is room for on-going research on Czech mission. It seems remarkable that there is a growing Czech international mission, despite the rather unfavourable religious situation and domestic needs. Still, literature on international mission from the Czech Protestant (and other in varying degree as well) churches is meagre and needs to be enhanced. My work is a pioneering work in a sense, yet it focused on one aspect (national identity) in one specific area (former Yugoslavia countries). Other topics could examine the mission theology basis on which Czech churches send and support intercultural missionaries, contemporary mission to Czechs and to foreigners in the Czech Republic, and the identity of Czech missionaries in other culturally proximal contexts, such as in the former Soviet republics. Furthermore, the appearance of more publications on mission in connection to identity, on patriotism and nationalism in mission, and on negotiating other national cultures, apart from the host culture(s), that missionaries encounter, would be useful.

When I retrospectively reflect on my journey of learning about the topic, apart from realising the limitations and a need of continuation, I gladly recall the encounters with the missionaries and others who provided the interviews, thankful that they spent time with me and opened up to me. My biggest thanks go to God as a deep appreciation of who He is and of the ways He has been weaving my life path, including my own missionary experience and my studies. It made me realise the need for readiness of us Christians to be prepared to be led by Him where He calls us.

Bibliography

Adeney, Miriam. 2009. 'Is God Colorblind or Colorful?: The Gospel, Globalization and Ethnicity.' In *Perspectives on the World Christian Movement: Reader.* R.D. Winter and S.C. Hawthorne, Eds. Pasadena, CA: William Carey Library, 415-422.

Anon. 2011. 'The Cape Town Commitment: A Confession of Faith and a Call to Action.' *International Bulletin of Missionary Research* 35:2, 59-80.

Anderson, Benedict. 1991. *Imagined Communities: Reflection on the Origin and Spread of Nationalism,* 2nd edn. London: Verso.

Bevans, Stephen B. and Roger Schroeder. 2004. *Constants in Context: A Theology of Mission for Today.* Maryknoll, NY: Orbis Books.

Bodenhausen, Galen V. and Sonia K. Kang. 2015. 'Multiple Identities in Social Perception and Interaction: Challenges and Opportunities.' *Annual Review of Psychology* 66:1, 547-574.

Bosch, David J. 1991. *Transforming Mission: Paradigm Shifts in Theology of Mission.* Maryknoll, NY: Orbis Books.

Brewer, Marilynn B 2010 'Social Identity Complexity and Acceptance of Diversity' in RJ Crisp ed. 2010 *The Psychology of Social and Cultural Diversity* Gichester: Blackwell, 11–33.

Činčala, Petr. 2002. 'A Theoretical Proposal for Reaching Irreligious Czech People through a Mission Revitalization Movement.' PhD Thesis, Berrien Springs, MI: Andrews University.

EVALUE – European Values in Education 2020 *European Values Study*. Available at: https://www.atlasofeuropeanvalues.eu/maptool.html Accessed 29 Oct 2020.

Gellner, Ernest. 1964. *Thought and Change.* London: Weidenfeld and Nicolson.

Giddens, Anthony. 2017. *Sociology,* 8th edn. Cambridge: Polity Press.

Hesselgrave, David J. 1991. *Communicating Christ Cross-Culturally: An Introduction to Missionary Communication.* Grand Rapids, MI: Zondervan.

Hiebert, Paul G. 1983. *Cultural Anthropology.* Grand Rapids, MI: Baker Book House.

–––. 1985. *Anthropological Insights for Missionaries.* Grand Rapids, MI: Baker Book House.

Hošek, Pavel. 2015. 'Discerning the Signs of the Times in Post-communist Czech Republic: A Historical, Sociological and Missiological Analysis of Contemporary Czech Culture.' In *A Czech Perspective on Faith in a Secular Age.* T. Halík & P. Hošek, Eds. Washington, DC: The Council for Research in Values and Philosophy, 13-42.

Ieda, Osamu. 2004. 'Regional Identities and Meso-mega Area Dynamics in Slavic Eurasia: Focused on Eastern Europe.' *Regio – Minorities, Politics, Society – English Edition* VII/1, 3-22.

Klingsmith, Scott. 2012. *Missions Beyond the Wall: Factors in the Rise of Missionary Sending Movements in East-Central Europe.* Nürnberg, Bonn: VTR Publications.

Kool, Anne-Marie. 2017. 'A Missiologist's Look at the Future: A Missiological Manifesto for the 21st Century.' In *Mission in Central and Eastern Europe: Realities, Perspectives, Trends.* C. Constantineanu et al., Eds. Oxford: Regnum Books International, 694-710.

Kozhuharov, Valentin. 2015. 'Christian Mission in Eastern Europe.' *Acta Missiologiae* 4:1, 45-55.

Kuzmič, Peter. 1992. 'Christian Mission in Europe.' *Themelios* 18:1, 21-25.

–––. 2017. 'Christianity in Eastern Europe: A Story of Pain, Glory, Persecution and Freedom.' In *Mission in Central and Eastern Europe: Realities, Perspectives, Trends.* C. Constantineanu et al., Eds. Oxford: Regnum Books International, 13-29.

Mojzes, Paul. 1999. 'Proselytism in the Successor States of the Former Yugoslavia.' *Journal of Ecumenical Studies* 36:1-2, 221-243.

Newbigin, Lesslie. 1986. *Foolishness to the Greeks: The Gospel and Western Culture.* London: SPCK.

Niebuhr, H. Richard. 1951. *Christ and Culture.* New York, NY: Harper & Brothers.

Roccas, Sonia and Marilynn B. Brewer. 2002. 'Social Identity Complexity.' *Personality and Social Psychology Review* 6:2, 88-106.

Slačálek, Ondřej. 2016. 'The Postcolonial Hypothesis Notes on the Czech 'Central European' Identity.' *ALPPI Annual of Language & Politics and Politics of Identity*, 27-44.

Smith, Anthony D. 1991. *National Identity.* Reno, NV: University of Nevada Press.

Stets, Jan E. and Peter J. Burke. 2000. 'Identity Theory and Social Identity Theory.' *Social Psychology Quarterly* 63:3, 224-237.

Stryker, Sheldon and Peter J. Burke. 2000. 'The Past, Present, and Future of an Identity Theory.' *Social Psychology Quarterly* 63:4, 284-297.

Tajfel, Henri. 1981. *Human Groups and Social Categories: Studies in Social Psychology.* Cambridge: Cambridge University Press.

Tennent, Timothy C. 2010. *Invitation to World Missions: A Trinitarian Theology for the Twenty-first Century.* Grand Rapids, MI: Kregel Publications.

Todorova, Maria. 2009. *Imagining the Balkans.* Oxford: Oxford University Press.

Trompenaars, Fons and Charles Hampden-Turner. 2012. *Riding the Waves of Culture: Understanding Diversity in Global Business.* London: Nicholas Brealey.

Volf, Miroslav. 1996. 'Fishing in the Neighbor's Pond: Mission and Proselytism in Eastern Europe.' *International Bulletin of Missionary Research* 20:1, 26-31.

Winter, Ralph D. 2009. 'The New Macedonia: A Revolutionary New Era in Mission Begins.' In *Perspectives on the World Christian Movement: Reader.* R.D. Winter and S.C. Hawthorne, Eds. Pasadena, CA: William Carey Library, 347-360.

Wright, Christopher J.H. 2006. *The Mission of God: Unlocking the Bible's Grand Narrative.* Nottingham: InterVarsity Press.

–––. 2010. *The Mission of God's People: A Biblical Theology of the Church's Mission*. Grand Rapids, MI: Zondervan.

Žeželj, Iris and Felicia Pratto. 2017. 'What Identities in the Present May Mean for the Future of the Western Balkans.' In *Shaping Social Identities After Violent Conflict: Youth in the Western Balkans*. F. Pratto, Ed. Basingstoke: Palgrave Macmillan, 159-188.